# STEAMING THROUGH WEST HANTS

Peter Hay

*Cover picture details are
given in caption no. 80.*

*Design - Deborah Goodridge*

*First published July 1989*

*ISBN 0 906520 69 X*

*Copyright - Middleton Press, 1989*

*Typeset by Barbara Mitchell*

*Published by Middleton Press
          Easebourne Lane
          Midhurst, West Sussex
          GU29 9AZ
          Tel. (0730) 813169*

*Printed & bound by Biddles Ltd,
          Guildford and Kings Lynn*

# CONTENTS

West Hants and the surrounding area in the final years of steam.

# INDEX

# INTRODUCTION

Four years have passed since *Steaming Through East Hants* appeared in 1985. Since then the principal change in the Hampshire railway scene is the introduction of class 442 electric units which arrived when electric traction was extended to Weymouth in 1988. This book portrays the railway as it was before the greatest change of all: the end of steam working in 1967.

The first section shows the old main line and its continuation through the New Forest to Bournemouth. Before the county boundary changes in 1974 Hampshire included the route all the way to Bournemouth and both the stations there, though not the line between them. Next we look at the West of England main line from Basingstoke to the county boundary at Grateley and this is followed by a separate section with pictures of the railway in Southampton Docks. Although Southampton is a port of great age its growth owes more to the coming of the railway than to any other single agency. The creation of the New Docks by the Southern Railway in the years before World War II is a much underrated achievement.

The last two sections of this book could almost be called West Hants casualties of the pre- and post-Beeching years. They cover the route from Eastleigh to Andover along the lovely valleys of the Test and the Anton, and Castleman's Corkscrew from Brockenhurst through Ringwood by which trains first entered Bournemouth. Lastly, and also closed, comes the erstwhile Didcot, Newbury and Southampton Railway in Hampshire, a lost cause for much of its brief life.

The introduction to each section is no more than an outline. This is because the history is today more readily available than it used to be, not least from several Middleton Press companions to this album. Besides them you may consult C. F. Dendy Marshall's *History of the Southern Railway* and the books of H. P. White and Edwin Course which cover the west of the county in detail. Happily 1988 has seen the 20th century volume of R. A. Williams' story of the LSWR which extends to the formation of the SR, itself now more fully chronicled than ever before. The DNSR is the subject of several detailed books. On locomotives, signalling, and rolling stock we are well served by D. L. Bradley, George Pryer, and the OPC History of Southern Wagons.

It is a pleasure to take this chance to thank those who have generously and with great tolerance helped me with contributions to this book. I must specially mention my old friend J. H. Kent and also the staff of Hampshire County Museum Service, as well as Southampton City Museum who have given me the run of their Associated British Ports collection. Lastly I am grateful as always to Norman Langridge who provided most of the tickets and to John Fairman and Neil Stanyon who read the proofs. There can be little doubt that the line to Southampton would have been altered to become part of the Southern Electric in the 1940s, but because of the delay caused by the war we had another 20 years to go "Steaming through Hants".

*Peter Hay*
*Hove 1989*

1. This pre-war view shows T9 class no. 708 arriving at Basingstoke with a stopping train from Waterloo. To the left is the GWR engine shed with the line to Reading passing in front of it. Just visible are the starting signals and platform end of the Great Western station. (Lens of Sutton)

# 1. Basingstoke to Bournemouth West

The twentieth century is not accustomed to see the line to Bournemouth as anything different from the western part of a trunk route, but that is not how it happened. Joining London to the established port of Southampton (like the lines to Brighton and Dover) was an obviously profitable venture to undertake, but beyond Southampton there was no place of any size to be the goal of an extension. So the London & South Western Railway was cool towards a local scheme to go on to Dorchester, passing "through a line of country which, comprehending the principal towns, is still comparatively unoccupied by a resident nobility, gentry, and yeomanry; and over land remarkable for its barren and unproductive nature". Thus read a public letter of 1844.

The man who first visualised the peace of the New Forest being disturbed by a railway was Charles Castleman, a Wimborne solicitor, for when the main line from London reached Southampton in 1840 he could see that West Hants could benefit from its extension. After flirting with the GWR, the Southampton & Dorchester Railway - popularly known as Castleman's Corkscrew because of its circuitous route - formed an alliance with the LSWR and was opened in 1847. At that date only Poole and Christchurch had populations exceeding 6000; it was 1871 before Bournemouth reached that size. However its population trebled in the next 10 years and doubled in the ensuing decade, being 37600 by 1891. Bournemouth's rise as a resort was not matched by any LSWR initiative until the 1880s when, under pressure from the inhabitants who were consorting too much with Paddington for Waterloo's peace of mind, a direct line from Brockenhurst to Christchurch was opened and Bournemouth got a proper train service at last. Bournemouth has never looked back and today has two trains an hour from London and several daily services from the North.

The land may have been "unoccupied ..... and remarkable for its barren and unproductive nature" but for the LSWR and its successors it proved to be the rainbow, with Bournemouth the crock of gold at the end of it. So we have that lovely lonely line through the New Forest, though the speeds of today's electrics barely give us time to savour it. At least modern train drivers don't have to worry about engines throwing sparks in dry weather and setting the heathland ablaze. The only victim of recent station closures has been Boscombe; its loss in 1967 was balanced by the opening of Southampton Airport (now Parkway) the year before.

2. Bridge rails on longitudinal timbers and the details of roof construction identify the GWR station at Basingstoke as a Brunel design. In this turn of the century view the near platform line ends in buffer stops but the far one, spanned by a drawbridge, passes through the west end of the building. The wide space between the platforms was because the tracks here were mixed gauge until 1869.
(Hampshire County Museum Service)

3. Having only three roads under cover, Basingstoke loco shed was often crowded and engines had to stand outside. The "Remembrance" class were all shedded here in 1955 including no. 32327 *Trevithick*. Behind, there was a GWR engine, their shed having been closed some years before.

5. Comparison with the previous picture taken five months earlier, shows change at Micheldever. The tracks are gone from the up and down platform loop lines and the former island platform has been reopened on the old slow lines. No. 34097 *145 Squadron* is passing through on an up parcels train. (J. Scrace)

4. In March 1966, LNER A4 class no. 60024 *Kingfisher* stormed south through Micheldever with a rail tour. The down platform line is to the right of the train. Eight months later *Kingfisher* fetched just £3250 as scrap metal. (J. Scrace)

6.  The platforms at Winchester were lengthened at the south end in 1965 preparatory to electrification. Besides cutting the southern connection to the goods yard (to the right of 4-6-0 no. 73088) they also had to dig up the platform to lay cables for colour light signals. (Lens of Sutton)

7.  It may be 36 years old with 1.25 million miles 'on the clock' but King Arthur class no. 30773 *Sir Lavaine* isn't giving in to old age. As it races past Shawford with a down Bournemouth line extra in July 1961, we can see the 1943 additional line on the extreme right. (J. H. W. Kent)

8.  The clean leading coaches of this down train passing Shawford are part of a Bulleid 6-coach dining car set with panelling carried down to the footboards. These sets were built for the Bournemouth expresses in 1947. Rebuilt Merchant Navy class no. 35028 *Clan Line* is today just as clean as its train, one of the select band of preserved locomotives. (J. H. W. Kent)

9. Allbrook signal box was provided in 1898 and stood on the down side of the four track section laid north of Eastleigh to Shawford. It served the access to the East yard behind the train. No. 34007 *Wadebridge* is on an up train and its coaches can be compared with the "luxury set" seen in the previous picture. (Lens of Sutton)

10. This GWR Mogul has come to Eastleigh from Salisbury via Romsey. The tail of its train is just coming off the branch and crossing the up main line by Eastleigh East Box, the up line signals of which are seen over the footbridge. No. 6345 is one of the 1923 series of 2-6-0s, once found all over the GWR on every sort of train.

11. In May 1963 the Eastleigh "Heavy Lifter" was the Ransomes & Rapier steam crane supplied to the LSWR in 1918. It became no. DS35 and is seen on the up through line at Eastleigh with its Mess & Tool Van (a former LSWR "Ironclad" bogie coach) headed by double-chimneyed class 4MT no. 75079. The locomotive alone has escaped the scrap merchants and is now residing on the Plym Valley Railway. (J. H. W. Kent)

12. No. B216 was the only Stroudley D1 class 0-4-2 tank rebuilt with a larger boiler, by Marsh in 1910. This August 1934 picture might be the last ever taken of it. When the boiler was condemned the locomotive was withdrawn in August 1933, and after some time was taken to the Works to be cut up. (J. G. Sturt)

13. Three weeks after the end of World War II, on 22nd September 1945, T9 class no. 313 called at Swaythling with a down train. The funereal condition of the engine, the white "anti-black-out" rings on the awning supports and the small letters of the station nameboard are evidence of six long years of war. (H. C. Casserley)

14. The down train headed by no. 76061 has not called at Swaythling but is passing the signal box at speed. Nevertheless the driver has shut off steam because beneath Swaythling's starting signal, the distant for the Woodmill Intermediate Block Signals between here and St. Denys is "on" and his gallop towards Southampton must be restrained. (J. H. W. Kent)

15.   An up boat train from Southampton Docks passes the splendid LSWR co-acting down starting signals at Swaythling in 1963. The engine is rebuilt West Country class no. 34096 *Trevone* with a 72A Exmouth Jn. shedplate.   (J. H. W. Kent)

16. The 7.20am Weymouth to Waterloo was a heavy train and regaining speed after calling at Southampton is proving no easy task for "Lord Nelson" class no. 30861 *Lord Anson* . As His Lordship passes St. Denys, there is rather too much steam coming from places other than the chimney. (N. Sprinks)

17. St. Denys once had a fine array of LSWR signals, some being raised to be visible over the footbridge. How delighted we all would be if the coaches behind no. 30120 on this Portsmouth to Salisbury train had been spared to run with it on the Mid Hants Railway.

18. Sometime in the late 1950s, SR type upper quadrant signals replaced the older ones at the south end of St. Denys' platforms. GWR no. 2214 is heading north with the 1.55pm train from Southampton Terminus to the DNS line. Being a "foreigner" it ignores the SR disc head-codes and uses the Railway Clearing House lamp code, one under the chimney denoting a stopping passenger train. (J. H. W. Kent)

19. In 1955 Southampton had no engine shed of its own but there was a servicing point just north of the Terminus station, used by Western Region engines off the DNS and MSWSR routes. A local resident was the small engine used on the Town Quay. In this picture it is no. 30588, a tiny machine which started life in 1906 as a 2-2-0 tank hauling one coach as a "motor train" and later rebuilt to the more conventional 0-4-0T form. Other engines on view are a GWR 0-6-0 and a "Manor" class 4-6-0, while the distant feather of steam comes from a T9 on the turntable.

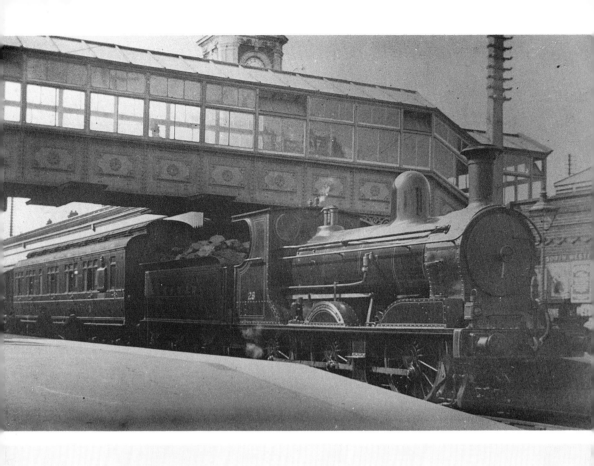

20. The Midland & South Western Junction Railway used their 0-6-0s for either goods or passenger work and here is no. 28, new in 1902, at the east end of Southampton West station. The first coach in this train from Cheltenham is a lordly Midland clerestory, one of several daily through coaches to Southampton from stations in the Midlands. Such convenient services continued to the last war, the 10.10am from Southampton conveying through carriages to Liverpool. (A. Vaughan collection)

21. The pillar of the level crossing gate marks the location where the siding to Southampton's electricity generating station crossed the Western Esplanade at the east end of Southampton station. On 4th August 1962 no. 30782 *Sir Brian* had only a short train and there were as yet no signs of the coming electrification. (A. E. Bennett)

22. U class no. 31795 with a BR chimney was super power for this two coach train setting off west under Southampton's much-photographed signal gantry. In the background we can just see one of the diesel sets which had made their appearance on local workings by 1958. (A. E. Bennett)

23. The down "Bournemouth Belle" accelerates past Millbrook capably hauled by no. 35012 *United States Lines* on 21st April 1966. The white dots are insulator pots for the third rail which is lying in the "six foot" ready to be installed. The two tracks on the right serve the Western (or New) Docks. (D. Fereday Glenn)

24. USA 0-6-0T no. DS233 (ex 30061) stands outside its shed at Redbridge Sleeper Depot on 21st April 1966. The vertical grab rails on the ends of the tanks were added during service in the Docks to improve safety. (D. Fereday Glenn)

25. No. 35021 *New Zealand Line* crossing the junction of the routes from Bournemouth and Salisbury at the west end of Redbridge station. The 1890 signal box faces across the tracks to the stone-built engine shed for the Sleeper Depot engine. (D. Fereday Glenn)

26. Pullman cars first ran to Bournemouth in 1890, but it was 1931 before an all-Pullman train appeared, running only in the summer until 1936. Pre-war the load of 400 tons was a "Lord Nelson" job. Post-war the "Merchant Navy" or "Lightweight" Pacifics were used. No. 35007 *Aberdeen Commonwealth* has just crossed the River Test and is approaching Totton on the down run on 13th March 1965. (E. Wilmshurst)

28. A feature distinguishing Lyndhurst Road station was the massively trussed covered wooden footbridge. Today's steel replacement isn't blackened by smoke from engines like the grimy "Merchant Navy" coming up from Bournemouth in August 1965. The Pullman camping coach was at the other end of the station. (J.H.W.Kent)

27. Pullman sleeping cars have never run through the New Forest, but in 1965 you could sleep in the former *Sorrento*, by then P45, installed at Lyndhurst Road. Perhaps try to sleep would be more accurate. The original camping coaches were placed at quiet locations, not next to a fast main line with engines like no. 34101 *Hartland* thundering past at all hours. (J.H.W.Kent)

29. This 1957 view of Beaulieu Road shows that the luxury sets built for the Bournemouth traffic were well kept. Did anybody ever try putting an air-smoothed (never streamlined) pacific through a carriage washer to see if it would help locomotive cleanliness? No. 34018 *Axminster* is heading an up Saturday train in September 1957. (D. Fereday Glenn)

30. As the 2.15pm Waterloo to Bournemouth passes Brockenhurst we can compare the roof contours of LSW coaches from before 1885 (in the Lymington bay platform on the right) and after, when Mr. Panter took charge of their design. T9 class no. 702 was sent new to Bournemouth in 1899, the same year as this photograph. (Lens of Sutton)

31. Sixty three years later the Lymington branch train stands at the east end of the up island platform. No. 30052 has just been refreshed and its driver is now carefully securing the jib of the water column. Once again there is a wooden trussed footbridge.

32. Southern Railway "harps and slabs" were used to extend Brockenhurst's platforms in 1936, although the three coach train arriving from Lymington in June 1963 will halt alongside the older part of the platform at the east end. The west signal box (closed in 1978) is on the right.

*Top right*

33. Although the electric services did not start for another year, on 11th June 1966 the conductor rails were in place at Sway as no. 75079 called with the 10.43am Southampton to Bournemouth. (J. Scrace)

34. Steel lattice replaced trussed timber for footbridge construction as the years passed. Although the 1898 map of New Milton does not show a footbridge, with more and more fast trains needed to serve popular Bournemouth, passengers' safety required one. This up train is headed by no. 34024 *Tamar Valley*. (J. H. W. Kent)

35. New Milton was a typical LSWR signal box of the "glasshouse" period (1884-95) with a large roof ventilator and a stovepipe chimney: these glasshouses get cold in the winter. Because it was so close to the up line its name was on the end as well as the front. In 1989 no. 34046 *Braunton* awaits restoration but in 1965 it was working the 1.30pm from Waterloo. (J. H. W. Kent)

36. How do you turn a Pullman car into a gypsy caravan? Make it a Holiday Coach. P46 at Hinton Admiral has washing hanging in the vestibule and casement windows in the side. What a fate for the dignified *Hibernia* bult by Cravens in 1914! Happily 35027 *Port Line* is still with us on the Bluebell Railway. (J. H. W. Kent)

37. Look at the leading coaches behind no. 34002 *Salisbury* and you will see how much British Railways' Mk. 1 passenger stock owed to Bulleid's SR designs, even though the body side profiles were slightly different. (J. H. W. Kent)

38. Workmen turn to watch as a rebuilt West Country pulls away from Christchurch in 1965. The "new" line to Brockenhurst passes in front of the lofty signal box of 1888, while the remains of the 1862 line to Ringwood curves away on the left. (J. H. W. Kent)

39.　　The ringed arm on the signal gantry denotes that the stub of the line from Christchurch to Ringwood via Hurn was only a siding in the 1960s. One praiseworthy feature of the Bournemouth and Weymouth services at that date was the external condition of the carriages: look at the polish on the red BR BSK behind no. 34088 *213 Squadron*.
(J. H. W. Kent)

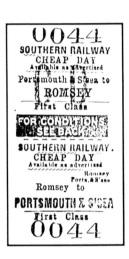

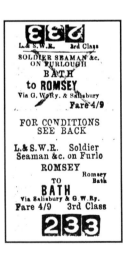

40.    The concealed part of the nameboard reads "for Southbourne on Sea", not to be confused with Southbourne in Sussex.    This is a through train to the Midlands via Basingstoke, calling to collect those whose holidays are over and who are bound for home in the Midlands behind no. 34085 *501 Squadron*.
(J. H. W. Kent)

41. West Country class no. 34024 *Tamar Valley* is on the up through line so it is not stopping at Pokesdown where there were four tracks from 1931 to 1972.  Today only the platform lines are in use.  In 1965 conductor rails have been delivered but they are the only signs of the pending electrification.
(J. H. W. Kent)

42. Presumably a signal check and not heavy-handed firing has produced the excess of steam and smoke at Pokesdown, "for Eastern Bournemouth".  With only 2 miles to go to the Central station the fireman of no. 73085 is going to have problems keeping his engine quiet when they get there.  (J. H. W. Kent)

43.   There was a period in 1965/6 when Type 3 (class 33) diesels shared duties with steam on the Bournemouth line and here we see the rivals passing at Boscombe, with no. 73014 on an up service.   Both types of motive power succumbed to the all-conquering electrics in 1967.   Having survived tramway competition for a long time Boscombe station itself was conquered by buses and cars the same year. (J. H. W. Kent)

44. Even though he has a clear road ahead the driver of Standard class 5 no. 73016 doesn't look very happy as his engine approaches Boscombe on the down line. Perhaps he still has to work back to London instead of finishing at Bournemouth. (J. H. W. Kent)

*Lower right*

46. The "tunnel bridge" under Holdenhurst Road in Bournemouth sometimes caused difficulties for enginemen, of a different kind to those caused to your author by the drinking abilities of a Locomotive Inspector in a pub down the road. No. 34001 *Exeter* was the first of the West Country class, here coupled with Bulleid brake third no. S3951S.
(J. H. W. Kent)

45. Boscombe station opened in 1897; the headcode displayed on the engine was not adopted until 1901, so presumably this picture can be dated as early this century. Adams 4-4-2T no. 416 was working a train from Ringwood to Bournemouth via the old line through Hurn and Christchurch.
(A. Vaughan collection)

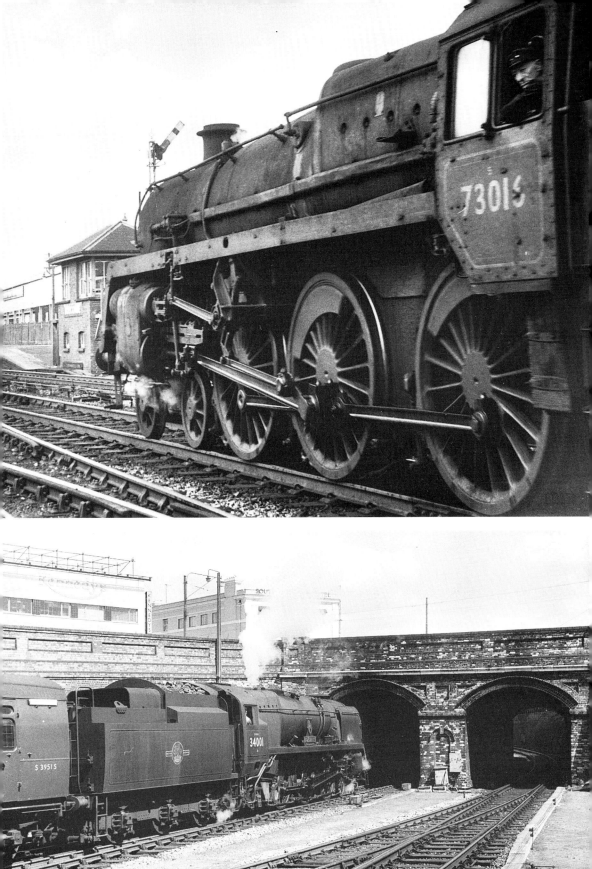

47. No. 34001 *Exeter* at the moment of departure. As his mate looks to the fire the driver will be leaning out of the cab window watching the porter on the platform. The guard with his green flag is out of sight round the curve and the porter will be looking to the rear of the train ready to relay the right away. In this expectant scene no. 75073 is the station pilot. (J. H. W. Kent)

48. The long down platform at Bournemouth Central (where two trains could stand simultaneously) provided a grandstand view of the shed yard. In 1965 there were three diesels visible, including Hymek no. D 7044, as well as steam of the SR, LMS, and BR varieties. (J. H. W. Kent)

49. Was this the source of all those gleaming carriages? At Bournemouth West BR thought it worth a sign saying "Carriage Washing Machine" for passengers who might be wondering.
Notices for the staff warned them of tight clearance inside the machine. (J. H. W. Kent)

50. With Bournemouth West station in the distance, no. 34093 *Saunton* backs past the signal box onto the stock of the up "Bournemouth Belle" on a June day in 1965. (J. H. W. Kent)

51. On 16th December 1953 T9 class no. 30289 was working the 1.20pm to Salisbury via West Moors and the Fordingbridge line. The train is leaving platform 2 at Bournemouth West with a Maunsell corridor third in green leading a pre-war 3 coach corridor set in red and cream. (N. Sprinks)

52. Somerset & Dorset Joint Railway no. 68 stands ready to leave with the 6.45pm to Bath on 9th August 1913. The coaches owned by the S & D were all non-corridor, like the six-wheelers heading this, the last through train of the day. Let us hope there was nobody on board who was going the whole three and three-quarter hour trip. (K. Nunn/LCGB)

**London and South Western Ry.**
787

*From*

TO

# WEST Bournemouth

53. The Midland/LMS presence at Bournemouth West was preserved latterly by 2-6-2T
no. 41312 of Ivatt's LMS design.  It is station
pilot as no. 34093 *Saunton* prepares to leave
with the "Bournemouth Belle".  As it stands
ahead of the starting signal, departure from the
station will be under the regulations for "starting of trains in advance of fixed signals".
(J. H. W. Kent)

54.    The passenger's view from platform 2
shows no. 80146 which brought in the empty
stock of the "Belle" taking water after its departure for London.  Bournemouth West could at
times be quite tranquil, though not on Saturdays in summer.  (J. H. W. Kent)

# 2. The West of England Main Line

One of the reasons why Castleman and his corkscrew were alienated from the LSWR for a time, was the latter's desire to push westwards from the vicinity of Basingstoke (where the Southampton line turns southwards) towards Salisbury and perhaps beyond. The Southampton & Dorchester supporters were fearful of LSW branches south from a Basingstoke - Salisbury line into their territory, perhaps to Poole and other precious sources of business. They flirted with the GWR whose Wilts, Somerset & Weymouth scheme was less of a threat and might give cheaper, shared access to Weymouth, in the 1840s the packet port for the Channel Islands. However the Southampton & Dorchester became part of the LSWR and the feared southward branches were never built, not least because it took until 1857 for the line from Basingstoke to reach Salisbury, after much argument within the LSWR. This was because Salisbury had already been connected with London in 1847 over a roundabout route through Eastleigh, so the direct line from Basingstoke was not going to bring much extra traffic. It was in fact part of the LSWR drive westwards to Exeter.

Neither then nor now was there much business to be gained from those windy miles over the high chalk of north Hampshire and indeed Oakley and Hurstbourne between Basingstoke and Andover were closed in the 1960s. The real character of this part of the SR is as a through route to the West. The gradients in Hampshire are easy and generation after generation of express motive power has romped along, free of the speed restrictions and general congestion nearer London. Back in 1906 the standard time for an express was 19 minutes from Basingstoke to Andover (pass to pass) for the eighteen and a half miles and many a crew, before and since, has lopped minutes off that schedule. Such exuberance was not, however, the cause of two bad collisions at Andover which are pictured here. In each case the same train was involved: the 8.10pm fast goods from Exeter to Nine Elms carrying food for the London markets. On 13th October 1914 it ran past all the up line signals at danger and savaged the up Salisbury goods which was innocently standing at the platform. Two years later and running under clear signals this time it was ambushed by some runaway wagons which strayed into its path. The new and massively built H15 class 4-6-0s heading the up Exeter goods reduced many wagons to fragments on each occasion but were themselves hardly damaged. Luckily there seem to have been no fatalities, as it was the middle of the night and the railwaymen about at such an hour took to their heels when nemesis appeared on the up line in the shape of a big 4-6-0 with a long train in tow.

56. This view west of Basingstoke gives a good impression of the high speed feeling about the LSWR line for the first 50 miles out of London: four tracks and lots of straight, just right for racing westwards. "King Arthur" class no. 30745 *Tintagel* is hauling SR 6-set no. 459 in 1955 but except for the numberplate, the electric headlights, and a different livery, this scene could be 20 years earlier.

*lower left*

55. At the west end of Basingstoke station a stopping train for Salisbury headed by no. 34051 *Winston Churchill* waits on the right, while a rebuilt Pacific approaches on the down through line with a train for Bournemouth. The upper quadrant signals, like their LSWR predecessors, were all worked by compressed air. (Lens of Sutton)

57. On the approach to Worting Junction no. 34082 *615 Squadron* is signalled from the down fast to the down Southampton line, the crossover connection being subject to a 65 mph speed restriction. That is why the raised signal is fixed on a lower post: it indicates a route subsidiary to that of the "down through to down Salisbury" signal on a higher post, to the left of it. The pattern is repeated with the down slow line signals; the lower arm relates to the speed-restricted route, in that case "down slow to down Salisbury". (A. Vaughan collection)

58. The little signal box at Overton is of an early LSWR style, commencing about 1870 when interlocking of points and signals was provided at country stations. Many of these original wayside boxes remained in use (unless there were some major alterations at the site) until the end of semaphore signalling.
(H. C. Casserley)

59. Steam railcar no. 12 stands at Hurstbourne on the Whitchurch to Fullerton Junction service. This smart looking unit was the final LSW railcar design and began working the service in 1906. Even on such a byway traffic outgrew its capacity and by 1914 it had been replaced by a small engine with two carriages, working push and pull.
(Lens of Sutton)

60.  At Andover Junction on the morning of 13th October 1914 the massive form of H15 class no. 488 sits meekly amid the remains of the up Salisbury goods, waiting for order to be restored.  It was so little damaged that towing to Eastleigh works took place as soon as the line was cleared.
(Hampshire County Library)

61.  Two years after the previous picture another H15, no. 490 this time, was involved in another destructive collision at Andover while working the same express goods.  This time the engine crew were blameless:  careless shunting was the cause and no. 490 finished up on its side in the soft trackside earth.
(Hampshire County Library)

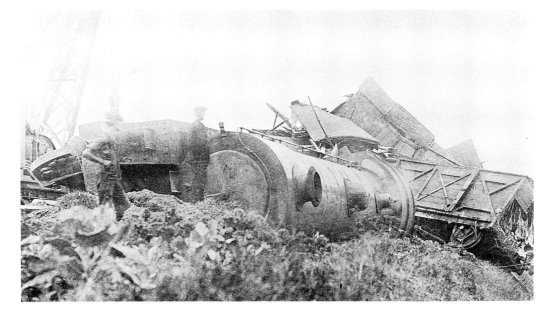

62. As we look west towards Salisbury, class T9 no. 30117 leaves Andover Junction with the 7.35pm to Eastleigh. The train is crossing the down main line with the up line platforms behind the signals. It was the last train of the day down the branch, rather early for Test Valley folk who wanted to sample Andover's night life in 1957.

*Top right*

63. The northern side of the up island platform at Andover was often called the Swindon bay, because Midland & South Western Junction Railway (late Swindon, Marlborough & Andover Rly.) trains were its common occupants. GWR 2-6-0 no. 7321 stationed at Swindon has just arrived from the MSWJ line. By the red and cream coaches at the other side of the platform the date is in the early 1950s. (Lens of Sutton)

64. The Gloucestershire Railway Society's special waits to leave the Swindon bay on 9th May 1953, appropriately headed by 2-4-0 no. 1336, sometime MSWJR no. 12 and the last engine of that railway in service. The GWR boiler was fitted after the old company was taken over in 1923. (N. Spinks)

65. Bringing us almost up to date, immaculately preserved Merchant Navy no. 35028 *Clan Line* is seen approaching the Dorsetshire county boundary with Grateley station in the background on 4th August 1987. (S. C. Nash)

66. Late in 1902 several members of the Docks Department staff pose with B4 class *St. Malo*; some docks engines carried their numbers only on the bufferbeams. The minimal cab was extended in 1903 to give the crew more protection from the weather. Notice the crease in the cylinder cover, no doubt the result of a tight squeeze somewhere around the place. (Southampton City Museum)

# 3. Southampton Docks

King Canute attempted to hold back the tide at Southampton; success was the reward of the Southampton Dock Company (1836-1892), the LSWR (1892-1922) and the Southern Railway. The pioneering Southampton Dock Company having difficulty in raising capital, sold out to the LSWR in 1892, and the railway set about reinvigorating and expanding the port. In this century Southampton usurped Liverpool's position as the passenger port for the best crossing to New York, and eventually attracted so many scheduled liner services that the Southern Railway was able to name 29 of its largest express engines after the lines whose ships called there. Even in 1856 the LSWR ran five goods trains daily to Southampton and the growth of freight traffic also benefitted from investment in port facilities, as these pictures show.

The achievement of the SR was and remains magnificent, though since the advent of the jet airliner some of the magic that used to invest Southampton has departed. Its heyday was probably in the 1950s when the strikingly modern Ocean Terminal was a suitably glamorous setting for the arrival and departure of everybody who was anybody, en route to or from New York. The strictly railway part of this was special connecting trains to Waterloo where, in the 1950s, the departure of the all-Pullman *Queen Mary* boat train was a major social oc-

casion. It's different at Heathrow.

The SR regarded its work at Southampton as an achievement rivalled in importance only by its great programme of passenger train electrification. In the 1920s it began a major land reclamation scheme to the west of the existing port, creating a simple and efficient layout compared with the hugger-mugger of curves and corners which characterise the Old (or Eastern) docks. One undeniable advantage of the latter was the ease with which one could enter and wander about taking photographs. By 1900 Adams' B4 class 0-4-0 shunting tanks had replaced the Dock Company's rather varied locomotive stud. They were an enduring part of the changing dockland scene until 1948 when many of them were worn out. Their replacements were quite novel: American short wheelbase 0-6-0 side tanks, stored in Britain but never used in the war, for sale at £2500 each. Eventually fourteen of them took over the shunting work from the B4 class. Southampton Docks thus retained its reputation of being the home of unusual locomotives, until the diesels came in 1962. Today it is part of Associated British Ports, and although freight traffic is heavier than ever it is concentrated at the Maritime Container Terminal at the west end of the New Docks. Only the *Canberra* and the *QE2* cruise liners are served by special Boat trains.

67.   Two other engines are visible as H15 no. 487 backs onto its train at the main marshalling yard of Southampton Old Docks.  They are an S15 on another freight departure to the right of the telegraph poles, and a B4 dock tank next to it.   The date is 27th September 1935. (Southampton City Museum)

68.   Passengers from the Channel Islands arrived at Southampton's Outer Dock (the first to be constructed, in 1842) and were soon on board a train for Waterloo.   On 10th June 1955, "King Arthur" class no. 30748 *Vivien* was the power for the Channel Islands boat train, here rounding the sharp dockland curve towards the crossing of Canute Road near Southampton Terminus station.

69.   No. 30070 was one of the American outside-cylinder 0-6-0T and is seen here in the Old Docks with the terminal for the Le Havre and St. Malo steamer services behind.   A hinged plate to bridge the yawning American gap between smokebox and bufferbeam is raised, but this 1955 picture pre-dates the fitting of grab rails on the tank ends and radio communication equipment.   As no. 21 *Wainwright*, this engine now lives on the Kent & East Sussex Railway.   Today the terminal building faces the very modern Ocean Village leisure centre.

70.  The Ocean Terminal, seen behind this Holland America Line boat train, was opened in 1950 on the east side of the Ocean Dock and provided an excellent setting for transatlantic arrivals and departures.  Increasingly superfluous as Heathrow took over its role, it was demolished in 1982.  The engine is no. 30773 *Sir Lavaine.*  (Southampton City Museum)

71.  We can see two rail gauges as the great task of reclaiming land for the New Docks progresses in the early 1930s, with a contractor's engine steaming past what will become Mayflower Park.  (In 1944, as the Allied liberation of Europe progressed, this area was a train ferry berth from which many engines and wagons were sent to France.)  Beyond the Royal Pier and the Town Quay the liners visible in the Old Docks are the first *Mauritania* on the left, with the *Majestic* behind. (Southampton City Museum)

72. The shipment of the LMS "Coronation Scot" train to the USA from the New Docks in January 1939, on board the *SS Belpamela*, was intended as a publicity exercise, but the outbreak of war in September marooned the engine and coaches in the USA for some time. (Southampton City Museum)

73. This SR publicity photo of the 1930s which shows "King Arthur" class no. 452 *Sir Meliagrance* at the head of a "banana special" was supposed to be in the New Docks sidings at Southampton, but was in fact taken in Eastleigh East Yard. (Southampton City Museum)

# 4. Secondary and Branch lines of West Hants

The LSWR first reached Salisbury from the main line at Bishopstoke (Eastleigh) by way of Romsey and Dean in 1847. Salisbury waited another ten years for a main line route; after 1857 the older route carried little more than local traffic, for the GWR line from Salisbury towards Bristol was broad gauge until 1874. The branch from Kimbridge Junction north of Romsey to the West of England main line at Andover was opened as a single line in 1865. Although it never outgrew its early nickname of the "Sprat and Winkle", the completion of the Midland & South Western Junction Railway's through route from Andover to Cheltenham in 1892 brought more business. The line had been doubled in the 1880s but it took the MSWJR some years to make contact with the friendly Midland Railway, at its northern end. Thereafter the Sprat and Winkle and the MSWJR provided a useful cross-country connection until 1958. Closure came in 1964, and the fishermen on that loveliest of trout streams, the River Test, were disturbed no more by the rumble of trains passing so close that even the fish seemed to know the timetable.

An earlier casualty was that real byway, the connection from Hurstbourne on the Basingstoke - Andover line, to Fullerton on the Sprat and Winkle. Its completion in 1885 was supposed to provide an alternative route between London and Southampton but it never prospered. It was singled in 1913, the meagre passenger service withdrawn in 1931, and total closure came in 1956. Latterly it was worked from the Fullerton end, the rails between Hurstbourne and Longparish being lifted in 1934.

A section of "Castleman's Corkscrew" has suffered a similar eclipse, mainly as a result of the present direct line to Bournemouth being opened between Lymington Junction and Christchurch in 1888. As Bournemouth grew, so did the importance of the shorter route to Southampton through the New Forest. The Dorsetshire line which connected with the Corkscrew at West Moors closed in 1964 and that ended the life of the older route west of Lymington Junction. I wish I could provide a picture of steam at work at Hurn on the long closed Ringwood - Christchurch link, but none seems to exist.

Purists argue that a true branch line is one that runs from the main line to a quiet terminus and if you accept that definition, West Hants has two: to Lymington and to Fawley. Lymington is the older, reaching the site of the present Town station in 1858. Extension to the Pier followed in 1884 and since then the branch has been a convenient way to reach the idyllic quiet of West Wight. There are still connecting train services from London but most people crossing to the Isle of Wight come by road and take their cars on the ferry with them.

A branch down the west side of Southampton Water was originally part of a local scheme for a short sea crossing to the Isle of Wight but nothing came of the branch until after World War I. That conflict greatly increased the use of oil for fuel and led to the first of Fawley's refineries being built, which in turn brought forward a proposal for a light railway to the main line west of Southampton, though local routing problems deferred opening until 1925. In the beginning five trains a day were provided but passenger traffic soon began to take second place to the oil business, and ceased altogether in 1966. Until that date a pleasant excursion could be made by taking the teatime train from Southampton Terminus (there were only two trains a day by the 1950s), coming back immediately from Fawley to Hythe. A short walk through the streets and a ride on the pier electric tramway brought you to a "motor boat service" which plied its way half hourly to Southampton Town Quay. You might even see a flying boat take off or land on the Water during your passage. Happy days!

74. The 11.20am Andover Junction to Southampton Terminus seems to have caught the
Chandlers Ford porter unprepared and he
runs up the platform with his barrow towards
where the guard's van will stop.   U class no.
31618 is hauling a common local train formation of the 1950s, a pair of the "single sliding
door" brakes with a "lengthened third" between
them.   All date from the 1890s.   The engine
now belongs to the Maunsell Locomotive Society and lives on the Bluebell Line.

75.    BR standard class 4 2-6-0s replaced
ageing LSWR and SR engines in the last years
of steam and here one of them, no. 76019, slows
to a stop at Nursling with a Salisbury - Portsmouth train on 22nd May 1957.
(H. C. Casserley)

76. LMS type 2-6-2T no. 41305 arrives at the east end of Romsey station in 1957 with the line from Eastleigh hidden by the train, and that from Southampton via Nursling coming in on the right. The signals are SR on a LSWR lattice gantry, while the water column with its brazier to ward off the frost is of the LSWR short type.

77. Both the outer and inner home signals for Kimbridge Junction are "off" and so is Dunbridge's distant, so this Portsmouth to Cardiff service, hauled by no. 30721, has a clear run. The point rodding disappearing into the grass on the right is for Awbridge sidings, laid during the war to assist the immense US Army stores depot at Lockerley, north of Dunbridge.

78. The Andover to Romsey line curving in from the right joined the Salisbury - Romsey line at Kimbridge Junction where U class 2-6-0 no. 31808 is passing with a mixed load of GWR, LMS, and BR carriages. The train is the 9.00am Cardiff to Portsmouth on 13th May 1957, non-stop from Salisbury to Southampton. The 1950s were the last years when Kimbridge Junction saw daily through trains to "foreign parts", like Cheltenham and Swansea. On Saturdays in the summer, their numbers increased greatly to cater for holidaymakers.

79. Among the charming features of Dunbridge station in 1957 are the deep-set mullioned windows, crow step moulding concealing the end of the lean-to roof, and curved wooden brackets supporting the awning. This train is the 10.30 Cardiff to Portsmouth, hauled by no. 31805. It will not be stopping to pick up the milk churns on the platform, where there are two high-wheeled LSWR barrows.

80.  Dean is nine miles from Salisbury, but in the 1950s local travellers were offered an erratic service with long gaps.  Many of the trains which did call were long distance workings like this Portsmouth - Bristol service which has avoided Southampton by coming through Eastleigh.  The flat platform awning on wooden posts without decorative valancing but having an oil lamp in a fancy casing is typical of the early LSWR, Dean being opened in 1847.

81.  In 1957, neither 25 years under the SR nor 10 years of nationalized ownership have brought many changes at Mottisfont.  Only the track is not LSWR; the train, the signals, the oil lamps and the nameboard are all of the pre-grouping type.  We can see the hand of the SR in the 1925 reboilering of T9 no. 30300 and the two leading carriages have been rebodied onto longer underframes, but this picture gives a good impression of how little things changed on the "Sprat and Winkle" line, before the diesels came.

82. This picture of Horsebridge shows many features a country station should have. Firstly a train, which is the 10.08am Cheltenham (Lansdown) to Southampton. In the foreground is the loading gauge at the goods yard exit, which is controlled by a ground signal beside the trap point protecting the running line. The headless post with a ladder is not a disused gibbet; it once had an oil lamp on top to shed a little light on the proceedings.

83. Warm summer air completely evaporates the exhaust as this vintage train leaves Stockbridge for Andover. Engine, carriages, and the glasshouse signal box are all LSWR-built although that company ceased to exist 34 years before. They were obviously made to last.

84. At Fullerton in 1957 a grass-grown track still leads into the branch platform to the left, used by infrequent goods trains to Longparish. This train is one of the through Southampton-Cheltenham services via the former MSWJR, which began in 1893 and faded out in 1958. The BR class 4 4-6-0 with GWR coaches called at all stations on the "Sprat and Winkle" except Clatford, a sad decline from the Cheltenham fasts of pre-grouping days running non-stop between Andover and Romsey.

85. There being no turntable at Longparish, in 1928 "460" class no. 0478 had to run back to Fullerton Junction tender first. Here it stands with its one coach train at Wherwell, the rail-less platform opposite being evidence of hopes abandoned for the branch. (H. C. Casserley)

86. This Officers' special arriving from Longparish on 30th October 1957 may have been the last passenger working over the branch. Propelled back to Fullerton by a T9, the leading vehicle is DS1, which began life in 1880 as the LSWR Directors' Saloon. (S. C. Nash)

87. Presumably there <u>are</u> buffer stops in the weeds beyond the red banner stretched across the tracks at Longparish in 1957. What a far cry from the busy days of World War II when this station handled thousands of tons of bombs for the RAF. (S. C. Nash)

88. The "Junction" suffix to Fullerton was dropped in 1929, recognizing the declining status of the Hurstbourne branch. A signal box at the Stockbridge end controlled the junction while the goods yard connections were operated from the covered ground frame seen opposite no. 30028 as it leaves for Andover. (N. Sprinks)

89. As well as the goods yard to the left of the train there appears to be a loop line running behind the platform at Fullerton and leading to the signal box. Both upper and lower quadrant signals were in use in 1957. The building on the left is the original Fullerton Bridge station. It closed when Fullerton Junction was opened in 1885.

90. Clatford station separated the River Anton (in the trees on the right) from the by-road linking Goodworth Clatford with Upper Clatford. The level crossing leads to a ford over the river, all very rural and tranquil but not, alas, destined to last for ever. Indeed a diesel scheme was about to displace the LSWR train which formed the 6.40pm Andover Junction to Eastleigh on 13th July 1957.

91. The teatime train stopping at Clatford was the 2.20pm Weymouth to Andover calling at all stations except Swaythling, and created by continuing a Weymouth - Southampton train as a service to Andover via Eastleigh. BR class 4 no. 75070 has a Bulleid 3-set of 1947 vintage behind the tender.

92. The train in the rain is the 10.10am from Southampton Terminus headed by U class no. 31613 and composed of GWR stock, the whole service running through to Cheltenham. It is stopping at Andover Town station on a sharp curve added to the original independent route after the LSWR took over the enterprise and connected it with the Basingstoke - Salisbury line north of the town.

94. In contrast to Holmsley, Ringwood station still had a well kept look in 1963. The covered (but not enclosed) footbridge is worthy of study, as is the variety of platform awnings. The one on the right seems to be shared with the goods shed. No. 76016 waits for the signal to be cleared so it can restart its Southampton to Bournemouth West train.

London and South Western By.

TO                                        787

# Holmsley

93. Like the daylight, Castleman's Corkscrew was dying in June 1963. There was little local traffic and the BR 2-6-4T collected few passengers from the grass-grown platform at Holmsley when it called with the 6.50pm Bournemouth West to Brockenhurst. Less than a year later it was all over.

95. "Line Clear" having been obtained from West Moors signalman, the train seen in the previous picture sets off from Ringwood, over the two level crossings and past the signal box.

96. Lymington Junction signal box had a life of 90 years, from 1888 to 1978. In 1963 it looked younger than its years because the main windows had been reglazed with larger panes, diminishing the glasshouse look. The driver on no. 30052 is leaning out to hang the tablet hoop on the catcher as he leaves the branch. A 40mph speed restriction sign refers to the turnout to the Ringwood line out of sight on the right.

97. A goods van stands on the line to Lymington's original railway jetty while no. 30052 pushes a three coach train towards the present Pier station, leaving its steam hanging under the roof of the Town station. The unusual roof and its gas lamps were demolished about 1966.

98. On 2nd June 1951 Q class no. 30548 was working one of the Saturday through trains from Lymington Pier to Waterloo. The ineffectiveness of the crossing gates as barriers is manifest. (R. Blencowe collection)

99. Booking Offices (now Ticket Offices) come in many forms but the example at Lymington Pier must be one of the crudest. On it is chalked "Please Book Here for Yarmouth I o W", so perhaps it was used for motorists who preferred to leave their cars on the mainland, unlike those on the left who are waiting to drive onto the ferry in June 1951. (R. Blencowe collection)

100. The architectural style of Marchwood station is best described as "Garden City Cottage", with a brick addition in front for the signalling probably added when the passing loop was opened in 1960. USA tank no. 30064 is not working wrong line in 1967; both lines of the loop are bi-directional. (J. Scrace)

101. Until the oil trains came there were no passing loops on the Fawley line, the whole branch being one signal section of 9.5 miles from Eling Junction, on the main line, to Fawley. The only water column was at Hythe, where M7 class no. 30040 has just been refreshed. Both the style and materials of the station were typical of 1925.

102. A block train of oil tanks in Hythe yard in 1960, the year H16 class 4-6-2T no. 30516 was brought from London to help with these heavy loads. Its reign lasted just over a year, for by July 1961 it was returned to Feltham, virtually worn out. (Lens of Sutton)

103. Between 3rd March 1958 and 5th April 1964 there was a halt between Hythe and Fawley for workmen at newly built factories at Hardley. It was little more than a concrete platform beside the track, where the evening train from Fawley, worked by the usual M7 class 0-4-4T, has called on 17th May 1958. (H. Davies)

104. The liberal use of concrete on the Fawley branch revealed its twentieth century construction but this train in June 1955 was decidedly pre-grouping: M7 class no. 30040, built in 1898, with three contemporary carriages. In this rural picture the future intrudes in the shape of the chimneys of the oil refinery which brought an immense upsurge in traffic from the end of the 1950s. The picture shows the second of the day's two trains, the 5.16pm to Southampton. The 1925 Railway Magazine article describing the new branch merely said: "A siding leads through a gate to the AGWI Petroleum Works, and the Calshot aerodrome is not far away. There is talk of developments in the form of a watering place, and perhaps a crossing to the Isle of Wight".

105.   There is a goods train with oil tankers visible as no. 30040 runs round at Fawley in June 1955, but little sign of the developments that were to come.   Fawley station has been demolished and the site is merged in the refinery complex.

# 5. The Didcot, Newbury and Southampton line

When the London - Bristol line of the GWR was before Parliament in the 1830s, their great engineer Isambard Brunel gave it as his opinion that Bristol might be a collecting and forwarding point for "all of the carriage of the market produce of the West of England which now finds its way eastwards from a number of different points". Right through that century the Great Western never quite gave up the idea that it was the natural line of communication between the West Country and London. The LSWR occupation of the southern shore of western Britain must have been a mild but enduring affront to Paddington. In the 1840s and 50s they tried in vain to block Waterloo's expansion westwards, with scant success.

The DNS scheme was something of a late counterattack, not in the sense that it was GWR inspired, for it had independent origins partly in Southampton, but because the Great Western supported it just enough to make sure it did get built, one suspects at least partly to annoy Waterloo rather than to make a lot of money. The DNS was one of those slightly improbable lines of southern England, struggling to make a living in a thinly populated territory and attracting a devoted following of railway enthusiasts in the process. The Somerset & Dorset is the prime example and like it, the DNS was born of a wish for communication with the Midlands industrial districts, avoiding London and the monopoly position of the major railway controlling the area, in this case the LSWR. (The MSWJR also professed the desire of reaching the honeypot of Southampton). In both instances the money for an independent line all the way to the port was not available and the promoters and their Southampton supporters had to be content with access over LSWR rails, having given the latter a satisfying fright. In the case of the DNS, the GWR got in on the act well before the line was built by consenting to work it on completion. Having opened between Didcot and Newbury in 1882, it took the struggling company another three years to reach Winchester with Southampton still beyond the reach of their money or their trains. Finally in 1891, the LSWR put them out of their misery by continuing the single line from the DNS station at Winchester (Cheese Hill) to a junction with its own main line just north of Shawford. At last GWR liveried trains were seen at Southampton.

The DNS came into its own during World War II and the pressure of traffic was such that the Wiltshire section was converted to double track. That ended at Woodhay on the Hants border and south of there new works were restricted to improving the facilties for crossing trains on the single line. Between Shawford Junction and Shawford, an additional line was laid to allow trains to run direct to the 1931 down local line which began immediately south of the station.

Loss of traffic to road transport and what might be called "facing the facts" brought closure to the DNS in the 1960s. Today Southampton's desire for an outlet to the north, independent of London, is satisfied by the 1848 Basingstoke - Reading connection which still gives access to the Oxford line to the Midlands, and by the 1856 Salisbury - Westbury line which carries traffic for Bristol and Wales. Like the S & D and the MSWJR routes, only long distance trains made the DNS anything more than a quiet local line connecting scattered stations, but it has its devotees who have been compensated by Kevin Robertson's books celebrating the railway. I hope this chapter adds a little to their enjoyment.

106. Block trains of oil tankers from Fawley to Bromford Bridge near Birmingham began in 1960 and were routed via the DNS line from 1962, to avoid Bristol. 9F class 2-10-0s like no. 92004 must have been the largest engines ever to run on the line, which for a short time fulfilled its promoters' dreams. (J. W. H. Kent)

107. The figure 0 which begins the number of LSWR 4-4-0T no. 0321 denotes it is on the duplicate list and near the end of its life. In its old age it has been attached to GWR coaches at Winchester (Cheesehill) and is ready to take them on to Southampton. The date is about 1902, before the Saxby & Farmer signal box was removed. (A. Vaughan collection)

109. Does the schoolboy alighting from a Didcot-bound train remember fondly his journeys over the DNS? This picture dates from the 1950s when GWR coaches, albeit in BR livery, were still common.
(Hampshire County Library)

108. Resiting the signal box revealed the Gents in all its glory; notice how nature has reclaimed the raw chalk of the cutting side in the intervening 50 years. GWR no. 2240 was shedded at Didcot and a frequent performer on the DNS. (N. Sprinks)

110.    Passenger services were finally withdrawn from Winchester (Chesil from 1949) on 9th September 1961. The removal of the awning indicates that they will not recommence the following summer, but freight traffic still continues with 4-6-0 no. 75067 heading south towards the later signal box.    Today the site is a multi-storey car park.
(Hampshire County Library)

111.    In happier days at Winchester, a Duke class double-framed 4-4-0 comes out of the tunnel with a pre-war train from Didcot.    The arms on the signal post to the left of the tunnel are the same as those on the right, that with a superimposed S being for a shunt movement into the tunnel.    (Hampshire County Library)

112.    There was no passing loop at Kings Worthy, only one and three quarter miles north of Winchester.    On 5th March 1960, days before the withdrawal of passenger services north of Winchester, no. 2240 was help- ing railway enthusiasts make a farewell visit to the line.  (A. E. Bennett)

113.    Latterly Worthy Down Platform which served a nearby Admiralty establishment was one of the busier DNS stations, but these passengers are mostly pilgrims to a dying line. Former glories can be glimpsed on the left where once there were sidings, while on the right the arm of a tablet catcher just pokes into the picture.  (A. E. Bennett)

114. In the spring of 1957, Hampshire began to see a most distinguished visitor in the shape of the record-breaking GWR 4-4-0 *City of Truro*. Released from the old York museum and renovated at Swindon its regular daily duty was the 12.42pm from Didcot to Southampton Terminus, returning at 4.56pm. Here it calls at Sutton Scotney, a wayside station in the middle of the Hampshire downs. On the wall of the goods shed a very gentlemanly notice says "Enginemen are warned of restricted clearance".

ENGINEMEN
ARE WARNED
OF RESTRICTED
CLEARANCE

115. No longer does the porter stand with single line token at the ready as a Southampton-bound train calls at Whitchurch (Town), though the buildings are as well kept as ever, and the subway joining the platforms is still open to those who wish to cross the course of the line. (A. E. Bennett)

116. The serious young lady with the butterfly net has placed her specimen bottle on the footplating of this GWR double framed 0-6-0. Such informality, and the labourers assembled beyond the train crew, suggests that this picture near Litchfield was taken during the ballasting of the line prior to opening in 1885. (Hampshire County Library)

117. The sign on the disused platform at Litchfield (*Hants* underneath was added in 1909) seems by its design to be one of the originals. Today the house overlooks not a station denuded of its loop line but the dual carriageway A34 road. (A. E. Bennett)

118. Burghclere retained its passing loop to the end, just a few days away when no. 75005 called on 5th March 1960. The house and bridge are still there and the trackbed is now a private estate road. This station served only the hamlet of Old Burghclere and a lime works, despite the generous provision of station buildings. (A. E. Bennett)

## DIDCOT, NEWBURY, WINCHESTER and SOUTHAMPTON

### WEEK DAYS ONLY

| Mls | | am | am | am | am | am | pm | pm | pm | pm | pm |
|---|---|---|---|---|---|---|---|---|---|---|---|
| | | | | | Saturdays only | | | Saturdays only | TC from Oxford. Saturdays only. | TC from Oxford. Except Sats. | |
| | 152 Oxford dep | 7 10 | .... | 9X23 | .... | .... | .... | 12 45 | 2 56 | 2 56 | 5 0 |
| — | **Didcot** dep | 7 40 | .. | 10 50 | .. | .. | .. | 2 0 | 3 35 | 3 38 | 5 55 |
| 3 | Upton and Blewbury | 7 47 | .... | 10 58 | .... | .... | .... | 2 7 | 3 42 | 3 45 | 6 2 |
| 6¾ | Churn | 7 54 | .. | Aa | .. | .. | .. | Aa | Aa | Aa | Aa |
| 8½ | Compton | 7 59 | .... | 11 11 | .... | .... | .... | 2 18 | 3 53 | 3 56 | 6 14 |
| 10½ | Hampstead Norris | 8 4 | .. | 11 17 | .. | .. | .. | 2 25 | 3 58 | 4 1 | 6 20 |
| 12¾ | Pinewood Halt | 8 10 | .... | 11 23 | .... | .... | .... | 2 31 | 4 4 | 4 7 | 6 27 |
| 13½ | Hermitage | 8 13 | .. | 11 27 | .. | .. | .. | 2 34 | 4 7 | 4 10 | 6 32 |
| 18 | **Newbury** arr | 8 21 | .... | 11 36 | .... | .... | .... | 2 45 | 4 18 | 4 18 | 6U41 |
| — | **62 London** (Pad.) .. dep | .. | 7H30 | — | .. | 10H 5 | .. | | 2 35 | 2 35 | 6 0 |
| — | **Newbury** dep | .... | 9 7 | Stop | .... | 12 25 | .... | | 4 32 | 4 32 | 7 25 |
| 21¼ | Woodhay | .. | 9 15 | .. | .. | 12 32 | .. | | 4 39 | 4 39 | 7 32 |
| 23½ | Highclere | .... | 9 21 | .... | .... | 12 38 | .... | | 4 45 | 4 45 | 7 38 |
| 25½ | Burghclere | .. | 9 26 | .. | .. | 12 43 | .. | | 4 49 | 4 49 | 7 42 |
| 28 | Litchfield | .... | 9 32 | .... | .... | 12 49 | .... | | 4 55 | 4 55 | 7 48 |
| 31¾ | Whitchurch Town | .. | 9 40 | .. | .. | 12 56 | .. | | 5 3 | 5 3 | 7 56 |
| 37½ | Sutton Scotney | .... | 9 51 | .... | | 1 7 | .... | — | 5 14 | 5 14 | 8 7 |
| 40¼ | Worthy Down Halt | .. | 9 58 | .. | | 1 14 | .. | Stop | 5 21 | 5 21 | 8 14 |
| 42½ | King's Worthy | .... | 10 3 | am | | 1 19 | .... | .... | 5 25 | 5 25 | 8 18 |
| 44¼ | **Winchester Chesil** arr | .. | 10 8 | E | | 1 24 | .. | .. | 5 30 | 5 30 | 8 23 |
| | dep | .... | 10 9 | | | 1 25 | .... | .... | 5 30 | 5 30 | 8 24 |
| 47¼ | Shawford arr | .. | .. | | | .. | | pm | .. | 5 38 | .. |
| 51 | Eastleigh " | .... | 10 22 | 10 34 | 10 50 | 1 37 | 2V 0 | 2Y 6 | 5 44 | 5J45 | 8 37 |
| 53¼ | Swaythling " | .. | .. | 10 38 | 10 54 | .. | .. | 2Y10 | 5 53 | 6 4 | 9 10 |
| 54¾ | St. Denys " | .... | .... | 10 42 | 10 57 | .... | .... | 2Y14 | 5 57 | 6 8 | 9 14 |
| 55¾ | Northam " | .. | .. | 10 44 | .. | .. | .. | 2Y16 | 6 0 | 6 10 | 9 16 |
| 56½ | **Southampton Term.** " | .... | .... | 10 47 | .... | .... | .... | 2Y19 | 6 4 | 6 13 | 9 19 |
| 56¾ | **Southampton Cen.** .. arr | .. | .. | .. | 11 3 | .. | 2V10 | .. | .. | .. | .. |

| Miles | | am | am | am | am | am | pm | pm | pm | pm | pm | pm |
|---|---|---|---|---|---|---|---|---|---|---|---|---|
| | | | TC Totton (dep 6 28 am) to Reading General; TC Totton Reading Gen. arr 9 7 am | Saturdays only | Saturdays only | | Except Saturdays | Saturdays only | | S | | |
| | **Southampton Cen.** ...dep | .... | 6 40 | 11 26 | 11 41 | .... | .... | .... | .... | | .... | .... |
| | **Southampton Term.** dep | .. | .. | .. | .. | 11E53 | 1P50 | 1P50 | .. | 4 47 | 4E53 | .. |
| ¾ | Northam | .... | .... | .... | .... | 11E55 | 1P53 | 1P52 | .... | 4 49 | 4E56 | .... |
| 1¾ | St. Denys | .. | 6 46 | 11 31 | .. | 11E58 | 1P57 | 1P55 | .. | 4 52 | 5E 0 | .. |
| 3¼ | Swaythling | .... | 6 50 | 11 35 | .... | 12E 1 | 2P 0 | 1P58 | .... | 4 55 | 5E 4 | .... |
| 5½ | Eastleigh | .. | 6 57 | 11 39 | 11 56 | 12 7 | 2 12 | 2 13 | .. | 5 0 | 5 12 | .. |
| 9¼ | Shawford | .... | 7 4 | | | 12 14 | 2 19 | 2 21 | .... | — | 5 19 | .... |
| 12¼ | **Winchester Chesil** arr | .. | 7 12 | | | 12 23 | 2 27 | 2 28 | .. | Stop | 5 27 | .. |
| | dep | .... | 7 14 | | | 12 25 | 2 28 | 2 31 | .... | .... | 5 32 | .... |
| 14 | King's Worthy | .. | 7 20 | | | 12 31 | 2 34 | 2 36 | .. | .. | 5 39 | .. |
| 16¼ | Worthy Down Halt | .... | 7 26 | | | 12 37 | 2 40 | 2 42 | .... | .... | 5 45 | .... |
| 19 | Sutton Scotney | .. | 7 33 | | | 12 44 | 2 46 | 2 48 | .. | .. | 5 54 | .. |
| 24¼ | Whitchurch Town | .... | 7 45 | | | 12 55 | 3 0 | 3 0 | .... | .... | 6 7 | .... |
| 28½ | Litchfield | .. | 7 54 | .. | .. | 1 7 | 3 12 | 3 12 | .. | .. | 6 16 | .. |
| 31 | Burghclere | .... | 8C 4 | .... | .... | 1 13 | 3 18 | 3 18 | .... | .... | 6 23 | .... |
| 33 | Highclere | .. | 8 11 | .. | .. | 1 17 | 3 23 | 3 23 | .. | .. | 6 28 | .. |
| 35¼ | Woodhay | .... | 8 17 | .... | .... | 1 23 | 3 29 | 3 29 | .... | .... | 6 33 | .... |
| 38½ | **Newbury** arr | .. | 8 25 | .. | .. | 1 30 | 3 36 | 3 43 | .. | pm | 6 41 | .. |
| 91½ | **62 London** (Pad.) .. arr | .... | 10 7 | .... | .... | 3V20 | 5 55 | 6 15 | .... | S | 8 30 | .... |
| — | **Newbury** ..dep | 6 45 | | .. | .. | 1 58 | | | 4 20 | 5 45 | .. | 7 21 |
| 43 | Hermitage | 6 55 | | .... | .... | 2 7 | | | 4 29 | 5 54 | .... | 7 30 |
| 43¾ | Pinewood Halt | 6 58 | | .. | .. | 2 10 | | | 4 32 | 5 57 | .. | 7 33 |
| 46 | Hampstead Norris | 7 3 | | .... | .... | 2 16 | | | 4 38 | 6 3 | .... | 7 39 |
| 48 | Compton | 7 12 | | .. | .. | 2 21 | | | 4 44 | 6 9 | .. | 7 44 |
| 49¾ | Churn | .... | | .... | .... | Kk | | | Kk | Kk | .... | Kk |
| 53½ | Upton and Blewbury | 7 22 | | .. | .. | 2 32 | | | 4 55 | 6 19 | .. | 7 54 |
| 56½ | **Didcot** arr | 7 28 | | .... | .... | 2 38 | | | 5 4 | 6 25 | .... | 8 0 |
| 66¾ | 152 Oxford arr | 8 23 | | .. | .. | 3 13 | .. | .. | 5 44 | 6 55 | .. | 9 13 |

**Aa** Stops to take up or set down on previous notice to Station Master at Didcot. Evening trains call during daylight only
**C** Arr 4 minutes *earlier*
**E** or E Except Saturdays
**H** Dep 10 45 am on Saturdays
**J** Change at Eastleigh and dep 6 0 pm for Southampton Terminus
**Kk** Stops to take up or set down on previous notice to Station Master at Newbury. Evening trains call during daylight only
**N** Second class only for a portion of the journey
**P** Change at Eastleigh
**p** pm
**S** or S Saturdays only
**TC** Through Carriages
**U** Change at Newbury
**V** 5 minutes later on Saturdays
**X** Dep 10 0 am on Saturdays
**Y** 4 minutes later on Saturdays

**On Sundays, Bus services depart Didcot Station 3 0 pm to Newbury Station; returning from Newbury Station at 7 55 pm by Newbury and District Motor Services Ltd. Passengers holding rail tickets to or from Stations between Didcot and Newbury inclusive may travel by these Road services without additional charge**

**OTHER TRAINS between Winchester and Southampton Terminus, see page 436**

Bradshaw's August 1959 volume included this timetable. Passenger services between Newbury and Winchester ceased on 12th March 1960.

119. Highclere station was nearer Burghclere than Highclere. Today the space between the platforms has been filled in, but even in the last days before passenger services ceased, the up loop platform looks disused. GWR Mogul no. 6302 is homeward bound to 81E Didcot. (A. E. Bennett)

120. A few turns of the wheels will take GWR no. 7327 away from Woodhay's modest platforms, across the infant River Enbourne and into Berkshire, leaving Hampshire behind and ending our story. (E. Wilmshurst)

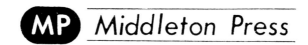

## MP Middleton Press

Easebourne Lane, Midhurst, West Sussex, GU29 9AZ
Midhurst (0730) 813169

## BRANCH LINES

BRANCH LINES TO MIDURST
BRANCH LINES AROUND MIDHURST
BRANCH LINES TO HORSHAM
BRANCH LINES TO ALTON
BRANCH LINE TO HAYLING
BRANCH LINE TO SOUTHWOLD
BRANCH LINE TO TENTERDEN
BRANCH LINES TO NEWPORT
BRANCH LINES TO TUNBRIDGE WELLS
BRANCH LINE TO SWANAGE
BRANCH LINES TO LONGMOOR
BRANCH LINE TO LYME REGIS
BRANCH LINE TO FAIRFORD
BRANCH LINE TO ALLHALLOWS
BRANCH LINES AROUND ASCOT
BRANCH LINES AROUND WEYMOUTH

## SOUTH COAST RAILWAYS

BRIGHTON TO WORTHING
CHICHESTER TO PORTSMOUTH
BRIGHTON TO EASTBOURNE
RYDE TO VENTNOR
EASTBOURNE TO HASTINGS
PORTSMOUTH TO SOUTHAMPTON
SOUTHAMPTON TO BOURNEMOUTH
ASHFORD TO DOVER
BOURNEMOUTH TO WEYMOUTH

## SOUTHERN MAIN LINES

WOKING TO PORTSMOUTH
HAYWARDS HEATH TO SEAFORD
EPSOM TO HORSHAM
CRAWLEY TO LITTLEHAMPTON
THREE BRIDGES TO BRIGHTON
WATERLOO TO WOKING
VICTORIA TO EAST CROYDON
TONBRIDGE TO HASTINGS
EAST CROYDON TO THREE BRIDGES
WOKING TO SOUTHAMPTON
WATERLOO TO WINDSOR
LONDON BRIDGE TO EAST CROYDON

## COUNTRY RAILWAY ROUTES

BOURNEMOUTH TO EVERCREECH JUNCTION
READING TO GUILDFORD
WOKING TO ALTON
BATH TO EVERCREECH JUNCTION
GUILDFORD TO REDHILL
EAST KENT LIGHT RAILWAY

## STEAMING THROUGH

STEAMING THROUGH KENT
STEAMING THROUGH EAST HANTS
STEAMING THROUGH SURREY
STEAMING THROUGH WEST SUSSEX
STEAMING THROUGH THE ISLE OF WIGHT
STEAMING THROUGH WEST HANTS

## OTHER RAILWAY BOOKS

WAR ON THE LINE
GARRAWAY FATHER & SON
LONDON CHATHAM & DOVER RAILWAY
INDUSTRIAL RAILWAYS OF THE SOUTH EAST

## OTHER BOOKS

MIDHURST TOWN THEN & NOW
EAST GRINSTEAD THEN & NOW

MILITARY DEFENCE OF WEST SUSSEX
SUSSEX POLICE FORCES

WEST SUSSEX WATERWAYS
SURREY WATERWAYS